10 DAYS
TO **DAD**

By
CHRIS HARRISON

10 DAYS
TO DAD

by

CHRIS HARRISON

Dedication

To my wife, thank you for the greatest gift ever.

Table of Contents

Opening

For those who decide to embark on the adventure that is parenthood, becoming a parent is one of the most fulfilling moments that a person can have in their life. For me, becoming a dad was both exciting and terrifying at the same time. Although my dad jokes were in peak condition, I was woefully unprepared to become a dad.

Yes, in this age of information, I was able to dive into every single "new dad" rabbit hole that the internet provided. In fact, I watched countless hours of videos dedicated to becoming a new parent and read an absurd number of online blogs, websites, books, and research articles; you name it, I probably clicked on it. My wife and I even attended online classes to "prepare" us for parenthood.

However, even with all of this prep, nothing could have prepared me for the final weeks leading up to my wife's delivery. It took exactly one pre-term contraction scare to make me realize that none of the resources provided a realistic sense of what I really needed to get done.

So, over the course of the final 10 days leading up to my wife's scheduled C-section, I decided to write down a few notes regarding what worked for me. Accordingly, I scribbled down the actions that I took to make the days leading up to the delivery as smooth as possible, mistakes that I wish I didn't make, and steps I took to provide us the space to focus on our little nugget.

Ten Days to Dad© is my way of sharing what worked well for me in the days leading up to my wife's delivery. Granted, there is no magical list that will capture everything that will be needed. However, I am hoping that this book will serve as a wonderful starting point if you need one.

As always, please consult your doctor or pediatrician for any medical advice.

Day Ten: Paperwork, Paperwork, Paperwork

Day ten is dedicated to submitting, reviewing, and finalizing any outstanding paperwork that you have in process with your medical insurance provider, FMLA and/or parental leave administrator, or any other loose ends that will require you to spend a significant amount of time on the phone. Seriously, you are on borrowed time and the last thing you want to worry about are pay or medical insurance issues that you could have avoided.

Day Ten Checklist

- Submit PTO (if needed) ahead of the delivery date.

- Set your "Out of office" message with the following:

  o "I will be heading out on paternity leave within the next [# of days] days. During this time, I will temporarily be transitioning work to **[Name]**. Please cc **[Name]** on any pending requests that you have. I will update this out-of-office note with specific leave dates soon. Thanks, **[Your Name]**."

- Submit a parental leave request (if you have not done so already).

- Review your parental leave benefits.

  o Review federal and state leave benefits.

  o Double check that your direct deposit accounts are correct.

- Review your medical benefits and the process for adding new dependents.

- Call your insurance company to understand how billing will work and when you can expect to have it.

- **[If open enrollment is live]** Update life insurance premiums.

  o I added supplemental life insurance to cover future childcare costs, college, paying off the house, and giving my partner the option of not working for some time.

- Update beneficiaries on all insurance plans.

- Sleep **[seriously, get a full night's rest]**.

  o **[Pro-tip]** Set yourself a bedtime and hold yourself to it.
    You are not going to be on your own schedule for a long
    time.

Notes

_____

_____

_____

Notes

Day Nine: Running Through the Plan

Now that you have gotten the paperwork out of the way, day nine is all about getting clear on your birthing plans and having a few challenging conversations. As you are packing your hospital and diaper bags, go ahead and start having these conversations. For the most part, I had the birthing plan committed to memory. Doing so gave me the ability to advocate for my wife. The cord blood and tissue banking threw us through a loop, and we were literally still debating if we wanted to do it or not as my wife was being rolled into the operating room.

Day Nine Checklist

- Review your birthing plan together.

  o Who will be in the delivery room?

  o Who will be in the recovery room?

  o Will golden hour/skin-to-skin be prioritized?

  o Do you want delayed cord cutting?

  o Will dad cut the umbilical cord?

  o What is the baby's name going to be?

  o Circumcision?

  o If you do not have a birthing plan, ask your medical insurance provider or OB for a template. The labor and delivery nurses will confirm your birthing plan once you are checked in.

  o Confirm who will be responsible for decisions in the event of a medical emergency where the birthing parent is unable to.

    * **[Hard topic]** If there is a medical emergency, should the birthing parent or baby be saved?

- Confirm whether you would like to store cord blood and tissue.

  o This can be an expensive decision to make at the last minute, so make this determination earlier on.

  o We stressed out about this decision as my wife was being wheeled into the operating room.

- o We asked ourselves the following question to help make the decision: "What regret do we want to live with? The regret of not having this when it could have been useful or paying too much for something we didn't use?"
- Pack your hospital bag.
  - o Place it in the car or near the front door.
  - o Recommended hospital bag contents:
    - ◆ Clothes for 4-5 days. I packed a bunch of old t-shirts and sweatpants.
    - ◆ Comfortable shoes that you can stand on for several hours. I was running around so much that my feet started to swell from the crappy shoes that I was wearing.
    - ◆ Shower shoes or flip-flops
    - ◆ Hoodies x 2
    - ◆ 8-foot USB cord x 2
    - ◆ Portable battery banks x 2
    - ◆ Laptop
    - ◆ Toiletries
      - ○ Shampoo & conditioner
      - ○ Body wash
      - ○ Arm deodorant
      - ○ Shaving

- I decided not to shave, as I didn't want any stubble to scratch the baby.
  - ○ Junior Mint candies
  - ○ Breath mints
    - Always keep two breath mints in your pocket. Once your partner is laboring and you are getting really close to them, the last thing they want to smell is bad breath.
  - ○ Jolly Ranchers
- Pack diaper bags.
  - o Recommended diaper bag contents:
    - ◆ Newborn diapers
    - ◆ Wet wipes x 2 packs
    - ◆ Diaper rash cream
    - ◆ Hand sanitizer
    - ◆ Changing pad
    - ◆ Change of clothes for the baby
    - ◆ Extra shirt for parent
    - ◆ Gallon-size Ziplock bags x 3
    - ◆ Snacks for momma
    - ◆ Clean bottles x 2
    - ◆ Swaddle cloth

- Burp cloths x 3-5

- Baby formula

- Portable bottle warmer (if you have one)

- Nursing pads

- Breastmilk storage bags

- Gripe water

- Hot Hands hand warmers

  - **[Pro-tip]** I used one of the warmers in the insulated pocket of my diaper bag to keep bottles warm.

- Place it in car or near front door.

- **[Pro-tip]** Have two diapers bags, one for each parent. Dad, keep your bag empty. You will be filling it up with goodies from the hospital, so pack that bag light.

Notes

_____

_____

_____

Notes

_____

_____

_____

_____

_____

_____

_____

_____

_____

_____

_____

_____

_____

_____

_____

_____

_____

Day Eight: Setting Boundaries

On your drive to the hospital tour, start thinking about the boundaries that you want to set with visitors to the recovery room and after the baby arrives home. The last thing you want is to have a bunch of people showing up when you are both stressed out, sleep-deprived, and easily agitated.

Day Eight Checklist

- Double check that you are checked in for delivery.

- Tour the labor and delivery ward, if possible.

  o Ask all of these questions:

    - How often do the nurses rotate?

    - Are lactation consultants available 24/7?

    - Will dad need to check in with security for a new badge daily?

    - When will the OBs visit?

    - How often will the pediatrician come in?

    - Will there be formula available if needed? What kind of formula is used?

    - Can you bring food into the recovery room?

    - Is there a shower?

      O Check if they require dad to wear swim trunks when using the shower. Yes, I know this sounds strange, but that was a rule at our hospital.

- Check out the cafeteria and the payment types that they accept.

  o **[Pro-tip]** Your partner will soon be able to have their first cup of coffee. Ask the nurses when you can bring a cup up.

- Find the delivery parking area or the general parking garage.

- **[Overbearing mother-in-law]** Ask your birthing partner if this applies to you. To clarify, you probably read that as, "debate my partner on whether or not my mother is overbearing." That is not what this means. Ask the question. Do not debate. Do not take it personally. For the love of all things, do not tell your mom.

  o Set very clear and firm boundaries here.

    - Will she be in the delivery room?

    - Will she be visiting during recovery?

    - What role does your partner want them to play?

- Your partner is about to be in their most vulnerable state both physically and mentally.

- Your responsibility is to make sure that your partner and baby have the best recovery and introduction to the world. This includes keeping any drama out of this experience.

  o If the MIL is making the birthing experience about themselves, it is **your** responsibility to have a conversation with them.

  o You and your partner are the parents of this child, not your parents or your partner's parents. Feel free to remind them of that.

    - Do not be a jerk and leave your partner to fight the MIL battle alone.

- Let people know that you will not have any visitors at all for the first week. This was a life-saver for us, as it gave us time to start adjusting to our new life and stopped some of the harassing texts from family members.

- For our greater friend circle, we let them know that we would be open to introducing them to the baby after month two.

Notes

Notes

_____

_____

_____

_____

_____

_____

_____

_____

_____

_____

_____

_____

_____

_____

_____

_____

_____

_____

_____

Day Seven:
The Final
Stretch

Your final week is here. Today, you will be focusing your time on three items: adding key labor and delivery information to your calendar, coordinating house upkeep and meal prep, and taking time to focus on your relationship.

Day Seven Checklist

- Add a Google Calendar or iCalendar event to your calendar with all of the details for the hospital and delivery.

  o Add the hospital location.

  o Add the time to be admitted.

    • If a C-section is scheduled:

      ○ Add the surgery start time and estimated completion time.

  o Add the doctor's contact and emergency contact information.

  o Add the recovery room location and floor.

  o Add visitor instructions from the hospital, as well as your visitor preference.

- Ask a friend or family member to do the following while you are in the hospital:

  o Water plants and feed animals while you are in the hospital.

  o **[Pro-tip]** Add them to a calendar invite and have them text you when it is done.

  o Meal prep while you are in the hospital.

  o Stock the house with any food that you like.

- Start sneaking pictures of your birthing partner over the course of the next week and through the first 48 hours after delivery.

- o Once the baby is born, you are both going to lose track of time. I snuck pictures here and there, and then had them printed and delivered to our house.

- o Sneaking pictures is also a way of showing the progress that your partner has made. This can be a helpful way to reduce the impact of any "baby blues" (Mayo Clinic Staff, 2022).

- Take a nice hot shower or bath.

- Cook dinner with your partner.

- Watch one of your favorite movies.

- Play a game together.

- Spend as much one-on-one time as possible.

- Want some serious points?

  - o Give your partner a foot massage... you will thank me later.

Notes

_____

_____

_____

Notes

(lined note page, blank)

Day Six: Practice Makes Perfect

By now, you should have your stroller, bassinet, crib, and car seat. This is a great time to practice using them all——especially the car seat and stroller. Try to get used to the "fully-loaded" dad walk, which consists of a diaper bag on your back, a weighted car seat in one hand, and a stroller in your free hand.

Day Six Checklist

- Check the changing table height.

    o **[Pro-tip]** You do not want the baby to lay too low on the changing table. You are going to be changing diapers a lot, so the last thing that you need to worry about is throwing out your back. Seriously, we ended up swapping out changing tables because we were killing our backs bending over too much.

- Practice using the stroller.

    o **[Pro-tip]** Practice locking the stroller wheels whenever you park or leave it.

    o **[Reminder]** If your stroller has a newborn insert, install it or bring it with you in the car. Do not be me and forget it at home.

    o Check that your stroller will fit in your trunk.

    o Practice using the car seat.

        ◆ **[If possible]** Schedule a car seat inspection with your local fire department or county.

        ◆ **[Reminder]** If your car seat has a newborn insert, install it, or bring it with you in the car.

    o Practice making a bottle with formula.

    o Wash the bottle and nipple.

        ◆ Sterilize the bottle and nipple.

        ◆ Make the formula.

- Warm the bottle.

- Check the temperature on your wrist (i.e., with palm facing up).

- Practice putting on a diaper.

  ○ I am a fan of the "practice on a friend's baby method." If you have a friend who is willing, practice changing a diaper.

o Remember those birthing videos that your partner told you to watch...and you never did? Go look at those now!

o Watch the following YouTube channels:

  - Dad Verb

  - Bridget Teyler: Built to Birth

  - Dr. Harvey Karp: "The 5 S's."

  - How to DAD (when you need a good laugh)

- Watch "hand expression" videos with your birthing partner.

  o I had to help my wife express colostrum and got a crash course at the hospital. This saved her some time as we split the work.

Notes

_____

_____

_____

Notes

Day Five: Getting Ahead on Well-Being and Self-Care

Understanding what recharges your batteries and what drains them is going to be extremely important. Start talking with your partner about what types of self-care they want to prioritize once the baby is here. Make a commitment to hold one another accountable for taking time to recharge their batteries as much as they can. Take the time to review content on postpartum depression (PPD) or "baby blues."

Day Five Checklist

- Go the ATM and take out $100 in cash and place that into your hospital bag

- While you are out getting that cash, stop by your local flower shop or grocery store. Pick up some flowers and your birthing partner's favorite snack.

- **[If possible]** Ask your medical provider for any content on postpartum depression (PPD) and read up on the signs of PPD.

- Talk to your partner about how you both want to manage stress.

  o **[Pro-tip]** Find ways of breaking your self-care into 30-minute chunks, several times per day.

  o My wife's self-care was a 15-minute hot shower with her favorite music playing.

  o My self-care was getting outside for 30 minutes each day.

- Let your partner know that it is okay not to be okay, but that you both need to be upfront regarding how you are doing.

- Make a commitment that if either of you needs an emergency break from the baby, the other will take over and watch the baby.

- **[Note to the dad-to-be]** Seriously, if you are stressed out, feeling under-appreciated or overwhelmed, or starting to feel down, talk about it. Talk to your partner or with someone in your support system.

Notes

_____

_____

_____

Notes

Day Four:
Payments
and Playlists

T oday is another day focused on verifying a few leave-related items and taking some time to rest.

Day Four Checklist

- Verify that deposits have been made to the appropriate accounts.

  o Check your expected pay dates for your paternity leave.

    - Adjust any auto-pay dates (e.g., rent, mortgage, utilities, etc.) so that they align with your new pay dates

    - Double check that the amount is correct.

    - Call your leave provider if you have any questions.

  o Create your "drive to the hospital" playlist.

    - We got pretty pumped up on the drive in.

  o If your partner wants music during their labor, download that playlist as well.

  o Sleep as much as you can.

  o Start being good about staying hydrated.

Notes

_____

_____

_____

Notes

Day Three: Setting Up for Recovery

Today, you will be focused on preparing some of the items that will make the recovery process a bit easier.

Day Three Checklist

- Install a handheld bidet.

  o Peri bottles are going to get annoying for your partner.

- Install a shower head that has a built-in handle.

- Depending on how your partner is managing their pain, you will want to set reminders for them to take their medicine.

  o We were on a 2-3 hour rotation for medication, so it was helpful to have our voice assistant-enabled device shout a reminder.

- Go ahead and start freezing some of the recovery pads.

- If your partner will be pumping, grab their storage bags, take a sharpie, and randomly add notes to the bags and place them back. My wife got a kick out of seeing some of the encouraging notes I left when she was up late pumping.

- Make space in the freezer for breastmilk.

- Change the air filters in your HVAC.

  o We had a lot of construction going on in our neighborhood, so this was a must.

- Update your "Out of Office" note with revised leave dates.

- Make sure that you have Metamucil or a fiber supplement in the house.

- Give your partner a back massage.

- Read up on diaper rash causes and treatment.

o   Ask your pediatrician for advice on creams to use.

- If you need to, make a run to the store and grab some baby formula.

- Double check your diaper supply.

o   We were going through 8-10 diapers per day.

- **[Reminder]** Schedule your pediatrician appointment.

- Unbox the items that you will be using once you are back home.

o   I made the mistake of keeping a bunch of stuff in the original boxes. Trying to fight with packaging at 3:00 AM is not fun.

Notes

_____

_____

_____

Notes

Day Two: Rest Up

Two days to go! On day two, prioritize sleeping as much as you can. Wake up late and take a bunch of naps. Get some decent cuddle time in and take it as slow as you can. Depending on timing, today is going to be the last day that you are going to get an almost full night's rest.

Day Two Checklist

- Sleep.

- Sleep some more.

- Cuddle with your partner.

- Encourage your partner.

- Laugh.

- Be selfish with your time.

- Stay hydrated!

Notes

_____

_____

_____

Notes

Day One:
Final
Touches

One more day to go! Today should be focused on running through your checklists and making sure that you have everything packed and ready to go. You are not going to get much sleep tonight. That being said, you are one day closer to meeting your little nugget!

Day One Checklist

- Make sure that you have a full tank of gas or that your vehicle is fully charged if it is electric.

- Have a back-up car or driver ready to go.

- Let your key family, friends, or support know that you are going in tomorrow!

- Turn off your work e-mail and chat notifications

- Reinforce boundaries that you have set with friends and family.

- Example text to send:

  o "Hi all, we're super excited that we'll be expecting the newest member of our family tomorrow! It is going to be a hectic day, so I want to let you all know that I won't be replying to texts or phone calls until later in the afternoon. I'll send one group text shortly after delivery, but after that, my focus will be on momma and the baby."

- Clip your fingernails.

  o You can easily scratch a baby. You do **NOT** want to be the first one to scratch the baby.

Preparing to Support Your Partner

Taking Notes

Take notes when the nurses and lactation consultants come in. Do not try to commit this to memory, as sleep deprivation is going to screw up your memory.

- Make sure that you are tracking how much the baby is feeding, pooping, and peeing. We used an app to do this, but you will need to keep track of this for the nurses and pediatricians.

- Ask the nurses who come in all of the questions that you are currently thinking are stupid in your head. Really, there are no stupid questions, and the nurses will not shame you for asking.

Breastfeeding / Body Feeding

This is going to be a huge stressor for your partner. Depending on their body, it may be more challenging than not. Keep in mind that formula is always an option. At a bare minimum, it gives the birthing parent time to work with the lactation consultants.

- What worked for me:
  o Verbalized my support of both body and formula feeding
  o Asked the lactation consultant for ways in which I can help my wife express colostrum

- o Asked my wife how long she'd like to try body feeding before transitioning to formula

  - ◆ Make sure that this is not coming across as an ultimatum, but as an opportunity to provide them with a break

- o Continuously acknowledged the progress that my wife was making

- Remember, there is no shame in keeping your baby fed with formula.

- We started off with formula and then transitioned to breastmilk once it came in.

My Rinse and Repeat Processes

For every feeding, I followed the following process:

- I would take the baby out of the bassinet and change their diaper.

- Once changed, I would hand the baby to momma, who would start to burp the baby and get additional skin-to-skin time.

- I would then clean the pump parts.

  - o I would reassemble the pump.

  - o I would take the baby so that momma could pump.

  - o Dad and baby would have skin-to-skin time.

  - o I would hand the baby back to momma once pumping

was complete.

o I would prepare the bottles.

- **[Pro-tip]** If you need to warm a bottle, running hot water over it and then placing it in your hand, armpit, or between your legs are all good ways of doing it. Of course, some methods are better than others.

o Depending on the time, one of us would then feed the baby.

- **[Pro-tip]** Have one of the nurses show you how to syringe feed in case it is needed.

o Burping happens throughout the feed and at the end of the bottle.

o Keep the baby upright for 30 minutes after feeding.

o Swaddle the baby.

o Put the baby back in the bassinet or have more skin-to-skin time with momma.

- Tips for responding to a crying baby:

o First, let me remind you that babies cannot talk from day one. Crying is their way of letting you know that they need some form of attention. So, stay calm and try to develop a process figuring out their cues.

o Here's an example of what I used when our baby cried:

- Is it their diaper? Check the diaper. Change the diaper. Burp.

- Is it hunger? Check for rooting. Feed. Burp.

- Is it gas? Burp for 2-3 minutes.

- Is the baby still crying?

  ○ Check the first three one last time.

  ○ Is the baby cold or hot?

  ○ Is the baby uncomfortable?

  ○ Check the first three again.

- While you are in the hospital, it is totally okay to call the labor and delivery nurses for support. You are not annoying them by doing so.

Notes

_____

_____

_____

Notes

Conclusion: Delivery Day

The day has finally arrived: delivery day. Hopefully, over the last ten days you have been able to prepare as much as possible. It is going to feel like a whirlwind, but just know that you and your partner are more than capable of doing this. There are going to be moments in which you feel like you are failing. This is normal. You are not failing.

You are going to be an amazing dad. Just know that you and your partner are doing the best that you can, and that is going to be enough for your baby.

Be patient with one another, be honest about needing a break or being too tired, and try to find moments to celebrate the newest member of your family.

I hope that you find some useful information in this book that can better prepare you for the days leading up to your delivery. Best of luck to you and your family!

Birthing Plan Notes

Questions for the Medical Staff

Made in the USA
Las Vegas, NV
26 January 2024

84930846R00046